MW00606596

Unless otherwise indicated, all scripture verses are from:
Copyright© 1992-2011 Logos Bible Software

The Holy Bible, Libronix NASB Version

www.connectingthedotsministries.com

Ver. 2

ISNB: 978-0-9832997-1-4

THE TRUTH

TRUTH

ABOUT

MARRIAGE

Rob and Lisa Laizure

This book is written for our children.

To our seven children and your spouses, here is a letter with love from Mom & Dad,

As you all know, we have been married for over thirty years. Since most of you are married, it is important to us to give you something lasting. We want to share something that will help you through life: marital wisdom. This wisdom can be difficult to share, because people say it is best to "leave and cleave". Newly married couples should not talk to their parents regarding issues in marriage. Yet, for those parents who have lived, learned, and strive daily to apply biblical principles to their marriage – wouldn't their experiences in God's truth about love and marriage offer wisdom to be shared?

There is definitely a fine line to walk as parents of our married children. We never want to get involved in your personal daily problems. Most of the time you are simply learning about each other and what being married is like. However, there are also universal themes that should be addressed. Many times newly married couples are confused. You need to know it's normal to be frustrated, confused, to be thinking and feeling things you may not have anticipated – it is okay. Those of us who have been through it are here to help!

We are not talking about the small, normal arguments that you have. We do not want to know the details of each spat you have. As parents, we know you need to work out your problems together without our influence. What you do need to know is how to love and care for one another in the midst of life's trials and tribulations. You need to learn how to respect one another and how to pray for one another. You need biblical truths to help you through what you are thinking and feeling. You need to know what is normal and that we have been through each issue you are getting ready to face in your lives together.

Each chapter will expound a new thought. It is our hope that these will be general principles that will help guide your lives together. Our desire is for you to love, adore, and respect your spouse. But mostly, we want you to live godly, biblically based lives.

When you realize that God was behind your choice for a spouse, then you can get on with living and learning the biblical response to your issues in life. Our hope and prayer is that these insights will be helpful to you throughout your lives.

Our first and most important desire is for you to understand the Bible, God's words to us, as the most important counselor you will ever have! When you read the Bible coupled with the help of the ultimate counselor, the Holy Spirit, you will be able to do what it says. When you come before God in humility, caring for the other person more than yourself, with a willing heart to change – then your marriage will flourish and be filled with joy.

Your testimonies also are my delight; they are my counselors. (Psalm 119:24)

Our second desire is that you get the counsel you need. We have made it clear to you that you are always welcome to come to us as your parents. Many times, we understand you might not want to talk with us and our only advice would be to find someone who knows God's Word. It is only then you will get the biblical advice you will need. There will always be people who will tell you what you want to hear or who will take your side of an argument. What we are hoping for is that you choose wise men and women who can help you look inside yourselves and see if the problem might be you. It is always easy to blame the other person and yet many times, the person having the problem might just be the problem. It takes someone who has wisdom and discernment to be able to see beyond just the facts.

> **Where there is no guidance the people fall, but in abundance of**
> **counselors there is victory. (Proverbs 11:14)**

> **Without consultation, plans are frustrated, but with many counselors they succeed. (Proverbs 15:22)**

> **For by wise guidance you will wage war, and in abundance of counselors there is victory. (Proverbs 24:6)**

We could think of no greater gift to give you, our children, than advice on how to live "happily ever after".

It does not just happen overnight, and for the most part doesn't even come naturally. Marriage is work. Marriage is a commitment. After thirty years of every problem imaginable, we still have issues but we have the tools to deal with them. It is to be hoped that what we will be giving you in this book are the tools necessary to be able to love God, love each other, and raise children who will follow in your footsteps.

This is our gift to you…

We love you all and are so proud of you. We are incredibly grateful for the men and women God has brought into our family as your spouses. We are truly blessed and we can see the hand of God in each one of your lives. We are amazed at the way He has complimented each of your strengths and weaknesses with a perfect partner for you to share your lives with.

Love,
Dad and Mom

Table of Contents

You Are Married To The Person You Are Meant To Be With

**The king's heart is like channels of water in
the hand of the Lord; He turns it wherever
He wishes.
(Proverbs 21:1)**

Isn't it amazing that your marriage began with a simple desire
to date a specific person? Have you ever wondered why your
affections were set on the person you married? Was it because
they were blonde or brunette, funny or smart? Why that
particular person when there were so many others? What would
make you decide to spend the rest of your life with the one
you married?

We would venture to say it was God.

Think back to when you were dating. You dated other people
other than the person you are married to, right? Do you realize
you did not marry someone other then the person you are
married to because God is in control and He had a specific plan
in mind?. The Bible promises that our hearts are in the hand of
the Lord and He turns it wherever He wishes. His wishes were
for you to marry the person you are married to today. If it wasn't
– He would have changed your heart and since He didn't – you
can rest assured you are with the person you are supposed to be
with. Many times in marriage – especially in the beginning when
problems start surfacing, we begin to question our decision. Did
I really know this person was like this? Why do we seem to argue
now, when we rarely did when we were dating? I thought my wife
or husband was more caring, more loving and definitely more
attentive. What happened? Did I marry the wrong person?

Please know those are normal thoughts and normal questions.

When you got married – all you could see in front of you was a beautiful wedding dress, a handsome bride or groom and vows that promised you would feel this way forever. There was the promise of moving away from the parents. Starting your own life in your own place. The world was going to be perfect. Then there was the honeymoon where suddenly you were thrown together in situations you had never been in before. Now you were in charge of a wife and she was your responsibility or you had a husband who was leading you around the airport. Now there were problems like bad hotels and hours and hours of layovers to get to your honeymoon destination. Then there was the usual exhaustion from the wedding, the newness of sex and the let down from months and months of planning. **Now…real life begins.**

With that comes the beginning of a learning process. What do I do when my husband comes home from work and doesn't want to talk because he has been talking all day to customers? Why was he so attentive when we were engaged and now he just wants to play a video game? Why does his job seem so much more important than I do? Why do we go to bed so early now instead of staying up late just enjoying each other's company? Why is the house always messy? Why doesn't my spouse want sex as much as I do? **And that is only the beginning…**

Welcome to marriage – the place where God has brought you. In this amazing union – He is going to teach you many things about yourself. Sometimes learning those lessons will be a difficult process.

So our advice is this:
Start by knowing the person you married is the right one for you. Yes, he or she might not be what you thought they would be – but you will grow to love the person they really are. Nobody is perfect and now you are on a journey together to learn what makes them happy or sad. You will grow together through exciting, fun, happy times and you will stay together through the rough patches. And through it all – thirty years later – you will look back knowing

the person you said those vows to thirty years earlier is the exact person God chose for you.

Be comforted in this – God does not make mistakes.

> **That they may see and recognize, and consider and gain insight as well, that the hand of the Lord has done this, and the Holy One of Israel has created it. (Isaiah 41:20)**

No Amount Of Nagging Will Change Your Spouse

When you get married, you naturally assume it will be easy to change your spouse. Those things that didn't really annoy you much before you got married – now you can't stand. What was kind of cute before is now totally frustrating to you.

Maybe you don't like that they read all the time or they don't clean the house like you thought they would. Maybe they would rather golf or fish than stay home on Saturday. Maybe they are trying to finish school and your idea of romantic evenings are now spent watching them do homework.

So – what should you do?

Naturally – you will want to complain. Don't you love me? Why is school or work more important than me? Why do you come home late from work? Aren't I the most important part of your life? You used to talk to me, you used to enjoy my company. Now you shut down and don't focus on me.

And the nagging begins…

Unfortunately – we have bad news – you will never change them.

But God can.

This is where you need to go – to God in prayer. All through your lives you will expect that when a problem arises – you will talk it out and then it will be solved. Not likely. You should always sit down and talk about what is bothering you to keep your lines of communication open. However, when it comes to true and lasting change – that can only come from God and the only way to get that is by refusing to nag and committing to pray.

**A foolish son is destruction to his father,
and the contentions of a wife are a constant
dripping.
(Proverbs 19:13)**

**A constant dripping on a day of steady
rain and a contentious woman are alike.
(Proverbs 27:15)**

These two verses talk about wives being contentious and the
visual is not a very pretty site – constant dripping. That is what
women can sound like when they go on and on about something
that is bothering them. The same could be true for men – if they
are constantly nagging their wives - it could also sound the same.

Our advice to you would be to let your spouse know what is
bothering you and then drop it and start praying. Many times
God answers our prayers immediately and other times it
might take years, but the best advice we can give you is that you
don't want a superficial change for a moment. You want a true
heart change that only comes from the Holy Spirit moving in
your spouse's heart.

Do you want them to respect you?
Do you want them to clean the house more to your liking?
Do you want them to cook more and go out to eat less?
Do you want them to desire sex more?
Do you want them to stop arguing about everything?
Do you want them to stop nagging?

Do you want to have fun in your marriage?
Do you want to enjoy each other?
Do you want to feel loved?

Then pray. Stop nagging and start praying.

When you realize you can never change your spouse then you

need to spend your time talking to the only One who can. The Holy Spirit living inside of you is the only source of power that will enable you to be loving, patient and kind when the change you want does not come fast enough.

> **But the fruit of the Spirit is love, joy, peace, patience, kindness, goodness, faithfulness, gentleness, self-control; against such things there is no law. (Galatians 5:22-23)**

Many times God is trying to teach us something. He always wants us dependent on Him. Asking for His help instead of nagging is a much more peaceful way to live together.

Make a commitment to pray more and nag less.

> **See that no one repays another with evil for evil, but always seek after that which is good for one another and for all people. Rejoice always; pray without ceasing; in everything give thanks; for this is God's will for you in Christ Jesus. (1 Thessalonians 5:15-18)**

You will be amazed at what God will do when you trust Him to change your spouse instead of you nagging your way to a superficial change.

Synonyms for nagging: irritating, troublesome, distressing, pesky, harassing and could also include being bossy and refusing to let things alone!

Trust us – that is not a good way to live...for either of you!

Run From Evil

Be very aware of your surroundings. The world will offer you many opportunities for distractions. It can be as simple as a coffee break with a co-worker, or a business luncheon with someone other than your spouse. You need to take desperate measures to guard your heart and your marriage at all costs.

Think of your marriage as having a fence around it and anything that comes close to it must be chased away. You must protect the vows you made before God and each other by running from anything that could possibly harm either one of you. Joseph in the Bible is the perfect example to follow. When temptation showed up in his life, in the form of a married woman, he ran.

> **As she spoke to Joseph day after day, he did not listen to her to lie beside her or be with her. Now it happened one day that he went into the house to do his work, and none of the men of the household was there inside. She caught him by his garment, saying, "Lie with me!" And he left his garment in her hand and fled, and went outside. (Genesis 39:10-12)**

He had the choice to hang around and flirt, relishing in the fact that this older woman wanted him, or he could remember his commitment to his God. Have you ever wondered why Joseph ran? For many people in this situation, they would say they did so because:

It was the right thing to do,
    They knew they would feel guilty,
        They would be afraid someone would find out…

And yet, none of those things mattered to him because the only thing that mattered was his relationship with God.

> **"There is no one greater in this house
> than I, and he has withheld nothing from
> me except you, because you are his wife.
> How then could I do this great evil and sin
> against God?" (Genesis 39:9)**

This is a great life lesson for you as you are in the world. There will be many opportunities for evil and yet the key to not succumbing to the temptation will be keeping your relationship with God incredibly strong.

Joseph loved God more than he loved sin. He loved God more than the fun he thought he could have. He somehow recognized that God's hand was directing his life and he didn't want to destroy the place where God was taking him.

That is something to always remember. God brought you and your spouse together and He has a plan for you and your children. Always remember that He was behind bringing you together and He has a life filled with blessings and joy, and yet all the good He has for you can be destroyed in a moment if you let your guard down.

Think of your own personal life with a boundary around it as you are in the workplace, school or gym. Guard yourself against anything that could remotely destroy you and your marriage. Be careful what you watch on television or the internet. Be careful of the people you spend your time with and those who may not have the same moral standards as you. Do what Joseph did and run.

For all the problems that this caused him; being falsely accused of rape and then thrown in prison – he had the one and only thing that mattered to him: his clear conscience before God. Because of his obedience and love for God, he was blessed the rest of his life. He got out of prison, got married, had two children, became second in command to Pharaoh and ended his life reconciled to his brothers and his beloved father. Why? Because he lived a blessed life because he made good choices.

King David in the Old Testament was an example of someone who refused to run away from temptation and instead ran toward sin. The consequences in his life, because of his sin, were devastating. His illicit affair with a married woman caused him to lose his child, murder an innocent man and his home was filled with turmoil until the day he died. The contrast between these two lives is worth remembering as you determine to make wise choices in your life.

> **Do not be deceived: "Bad company corrupts good morals."**
> **(1 Corinthians 15:33)**

Always remember to respond as Joseph did:

> **"How then could I do this great evil and sin against God?" (Genesis 39:9)**

Protect the most precious gift God has given you – your spouse.
Make sure they are your best friend.
Make sure your time is spent with them alone – go on a date or out of town for the weekend.
Keep your guard up against any evil that could possibly destroy what God has given you.
Have eyes for them only.

Enjoy one another so that nothing outside of that fence remotely entices you.
RUN…RUN…RUN

> **Let your eyes look directly ahead and let your gaze be fixed straight in front of you.**
> **(Proverbs 4:25)**

**Turn away my eyes from looking at vanity,
and revive me in Your ways. (Psalm 119:37)**

You Can Agree
To Disagree

When you get married, it is best to recognize you are two different people with two different ways of thinking. You have both been raised differently. One of you will want to save money and the other will want to spend it. One will like to go out to the movies and the other will want to stay home. One will be used to staying up late and the other will like to go to bed early. You have both been raised in two different homes and environments and you will both bring different ways of thinking into your marriage.

The key will be to recognize that if you both do not agree on something – sometimes it is okay to agree to disagree. As you grow in your marriage – you will begin to get to know each other so well that you will know what the other person is thinking. When this begins to happen, in order to have peace in your marriage – you will learn when and how to bring up subjects that you know the other person might think differently about.

Pick your battles wisely. If you know something bothers your spouse – do not antagonize them. Your best bet is always to pray for them. Pray for what you are planning to discuss and pray for God to turn either one of your hearts to where He wants you. We have made it a policy when one of us does not fully agree with something then we will not do it until God changes the other person's heart. That turns your dependence where it should be – on God.

When you don't agree on something – don't argue about it. Drop it and pray about it. Sometimes when we are tired or there is stress at work or school – things look bleaker than they really are. That is why many times it is best to just agree to disagree and get some sleep. When the morning comes – it is easier to have a new, fresh perspective on what the issue was the night before.

Remember that God alone changes the hearts of His people. Refuse to fight and argue about things that really don't matter. The key is to remember that a great marriage means caring about the other person more than yourself. Be there to listen, talk and try to understand your spouse and what they are saying, but if by the end of your conversation you disagree – then move on. In the end – God may be trying to teach you something and change your way of thinking instead of your spouse.

A perfect example of this in our lives happened when we wanted to buy some property in Montana. As the time got closer to close the deal, Mom was feeling more and more uncomfortable about the land, but I still felt it was something we should do. So, instead of arguing, Mom started praying. The day we were to close on the property – Mom was on one side of the wall (our bedroom) and I was on the other side (our office) and she began to pray that if God did not want us to buy this property that He would change my heart. Something started to stir in me. Suddenly, I didn't feel as comfortable about buying the land and I opened the door and told Mom, "I don't think we should buy this property." She thought it was funny that it was really that easy – she prayed that God would change my heart and He actually did!

When we get this – it will change our lives and our marriages. When we trust that God is the only One who moves on hearts and minds, then we can rest that He will do that on His timing and in His way. For Mom, it was a great reminder that God cared deeply for even the little things. Her faith grew because she saw that her job was to pray and it was God's job to change the situation.

God is a God of peace. Married life should be fun – free from chaos and stress and it should be the one place you could turn to for rest. If you are constantly in turmoil – then get some help to learn how to disagree without destroying your relationship. Marriage should be a safe, fun place to be. It takes two of you to get there!

Think about the worst argument you have had in your marriage. Now think on how the disagreement could have been handled being Spirit filled. What if:

You go to your spouse in the spirit of love.
You sit down to talk with joy in your heart because God is in the midst.
You strive to make the outcome one of peace.
You are patient and speaking with kindness.
Your words are gentle.
Your tone is one that is self controlled.

> **But if you are led by the Spirit, you are not under the Law. Now the deeds of the flesh are evident, which are: immorality, impurity, sensuality, idolatry, sorcery, enmities, strife, jealousy, outbursts of anger, disputes, dissensions, factions, envying, drunkenness, carousing, and things like these, of which I forewarn you, just as I have forewarned you, that those who practice such things will not inherit the kingdom of God. But the fruit of the Spirit is love, joy, peace, patience, kindness, goodness, faithfulness, gentleness, self-control; against such things there is no law. (Galatians 5:18-23)**

And in the end – there is no turmoil because you know that disagreements are not a bad thing – they are there to help you get to know one another and teach you to care for the other person.

Most arguments are filled with anger, frustration, yelling, and basically wanting the other person to do what you want. Unfortunately – that is no way to settle a disagreement. Each person should learn to listen to the other – present your side and let your spouse respond. If you cannot agree – **then stop and pray for what God wants** – not what you want.

*Refuse to argue. (we will say that again: REFUSE TO ARGUE!)
If you feel anger – walk away until you calm down!*

Care more for your spouse than you do winning an argument.

*Remember your spouse has outside pressure from work or school
and your home must be a place of peacefulness.*

*When you need to talk – make sure you are well rested and you
are not there to talk your spouse into your way of thinking.*

Always pray before you talk so the outcome will be God driven.

*Recognize your spouse needs to feel the freedom to talk to you
without feeling judged.*

*Remember – your spouse needs to be able to talk to you without
being afraid.*

God's Roles Are The Key To A Great Marriage

Marriage is like a football team. Some men are on offense and some are on defense. There is a quarterback and a defensive end, a long snapper and a tight end. Each person has their own job to do for the team to be successful. The team would be a disaster if the kicker decided he wanted to be the lineman. It wouldn't work. Each team member would experience great frustration when someone refuses to do their part to make the team successful.

The same is true in marriage. When God created the institution of marriage, He did so with a plan in mind. Each person would have their own roles and their own jobs. Along with that, each would be responsible to live their own life guided by the Holy Spirit who would then produce the fruits needed to make the marriage work. The key is making sure you are walking by His Spirit each day.

For you as the husband:

> **Husbands, love your wives, just as Christ also loved the church and gave Himself up for her. (Ephesians 5:25)**

God's greatest role for you, as a husband, is to love your wife. That is easy to say and yet in practical day to day living – what does that mean? Unfortunately, 1 Corinthians has been so over used that we tend to forget how that plays out in our daily lives.

The Bible says this about love:

> **Love is patient, love is kind and is not jealous; love does not brag and is not arrogant, does not act unbecomingly;**

**it does not seek its own, is not
provoked, does not take into account
a wrong suffered, does not rejoice in
unrighteousness, but rejoices with the
truth; bears all things, believes all things,
hopes all things, endures all things. (1
Corinthians 13:4-7)**

Now, think about these traits as you think about how you treat your wife.

Are you **patient** with her when she is in a bad mood or if the house isn't clean? Are you patient with her when dinner isn't on time or the bills haven't been paid yet?

Are you **kind** to her? Do you say nice things to her and compliment her? Do you take the kids for the day so she can go out with her friends or go shopping?

Are you **jealous**? Do you worry about where your wife is during the day? Do you question what she has been doing?

Do you act **unbecomingly**? How do you treat your wife around others or in your own home? Synonyms for this word are improper or inappropriate. Are you respectful of her?

Do you **"seek your own"**? Is your life more about you or about your wife? Your job as a husband is to care more for her and her needs than your own.

Are you **"easily provoked"**? Do you find yourself annoyed or irritated with your wife?

Do you take into account a **"wrong suffered"** and hold on to it?

The Bible makes it clear as a husband your role is to love your wife like Christ loved us. He died for us. He gave everything up for us. That is your job and because it is difficult to love your wife like that – you must be reading His Word daily and growing in your faith.

You can only produce this kind of love by the power of the Holy Spirit. When you recognize you are being impatient or jealous or selfish or frustrated – you must confess it to God and ask that He change you from the inside. This kind of love can only come from His Spirit working in your life.

For you as the wife:

> **Wives, be subject to your own husbands, as to the Lord. For the husband is the head of the wife, as Christ also is the head of the church, He Himself being the Savior of the body. But as the church is subject to Christ, so also the wives ought to be to their husbands in everything. (Ephesians 5:22-24)**

> **Nevertheless, each individual among you also is to love his own wife even as himself, and the wife must see to it that she respects her husband. (Ephesians 5:33)**

To make your marriage work like it should – there has to be a hierarchy. Just like on a team – there has to be a coach. In the government there is a President. In your business – there must be a boss. This doesn't mean that one is more important than the other – it just means their jobs are different.

A coach will take advice from his players. The President will take advice from his Vice President or Senators. In your company, hopefully your boss would get the input of his employees to better understand a more effective way to run his business. Someone always has to have the final say in a matter and in any team, government or office; there would be chaos if nobody had the authority to make a final decision.

That is why God has given you, as the wife, the role of subjecting yourself to your husband. Many women are frightened at this thought for fear of being taken advantage of. Many men can misconstrue this verse and give themselves a faulty sense of what their role as a husband should be. But if you put the two God given roles together – your husband's love will be a godly love that only produces safety and security for you. He will love you and trust you and ask for your advice. He will care more for your opinions than his own. Instead of lording it over you as the boss – he will allow you to come along side of him as his greatest source of help.

A beautiful picture of this is in **Proverbs 31**

The heart of her husband trusts in her,

She does him good and not evil all the days of her life.

She looks for wool and flax and works with her hands in delight.

She is like merchant ships; she brings her food from afar. She rises also while it is still night and gives food to her household and portions to her maidens.

She considers a field and buys it; from her earnings she plants a vineyard. She girds herself with strength and makes her arms strong. She senses that her gain is good; her lamp does not go out at night. She stretches out her hands to the distaff, and her hands grasp the spindle.

She extends her hand to the poor, and she stretches out her hands to the needy. She is not afraid of the snow for her household, for all her household are clothed with scarlet. She makes coverings for herself; her clothing is fine linen and purple.

Her husband is known in the gates, when he sits among the

elders of the land.

She makes linen garments and sells them, and supplies belts to the tradesmen.

Strength and dignity are her clothing,

And she smiles at the future. She opens her mouth in wisdom,

And the teaching of kindness is on her tongue.

She looks well to the ways of her household, and does not eat the bread of idleness.

Her children rise up and bless her;

Her husband also, and he praises her, saying: "Many daughters have done nobly, but you excel them all."

Charm is deceitful and beauty is vain, But a woman who fears the Lord, she shall be praised.

What an amazing, beautiful picture of a marriage and how incredibly important your role as a wife. Your husband should be proud of you for your godly qualities. You speak kindness, you are busy taking care of your household and your children, and your husband will have a great reputation because of who you are as his wife. You stand behind your husband and his decisions, you speak wisdom to those around you, and your husband completely trusts you. You are his greatest asset.

The second part of your role is respecting your husband. Do not talk about him in a negative way to others. Do not demean him in front of others. Refuse to argue or counter him when people are around. He must know you are his greatest fan.

Now, with these roles in mind – think about what an incredible marriage you could have when both of you are functioning in your God given roles. If your husband loves you with the love of Christ and is willing to give up everything, including his own rights, for you and then you walk beside him with respect – that is when you will have the marriage God has designed for you.

Don't Take Life
Too Seriously

Life is filled with ups and downs and the best advice we can give you is to learn how to be joyful even in the difficult times. When you recognize God's hand in your life no matter what the situation – you don't have to fall apart. The key to a great marriage is knowing that God is in control. Remember He is always moving you to a closer relationship with Him, first, and then a stronger more durable relationship with your spouse.

All through life there will be difficulties – that is a given. The key will be learning how to deal with what comes your way. It might be financial or relational and then when children arrive on the scene that brings another added stress! The best advice we can give you is to look at each problem that comes your way with this question, "What is God trying to teach me?"

All your lives, He wants you to learn how to trust Him. Most times, the only way He can do that is to put you in situations that seem difficult and painful. No money for the rent? He wants you to go to Him and trust His provision for you. An argument with your spouse? He wants you to pray that HE will change and soften both your hearts. Children problems? He wants you to know that your children are His and He will take them where they need to be for them to have a deeper relationship with Him.

Once you realize that most things in life are really out of your control – the easier it is to sit back, pray, do what God calls you to do and then just wait to see what He will do. Therein lies the peace of God. That is how you can enjoy your life together; refuse to take things too seriously. God is moving you into a deeper relationship with Him. You can smile when difficult moments arise, for in them you know He has a purpose.

SO....
SIT BACK AND ENJOY THE RIDE!

Before Grandpa Laizure passed away, the last audible words spoken that I (Dad) heard were:

"I took life too serious..."

Have snowball fights (preferably without getting all the girls wet), go on vacation, go out to dinner and the movies. Go to the park and feed the ducks, coach Little League, enjoy the time you have at home and take pleasure in your work. Life is so short. This may be hard to imagine at your age, but trust us...you all grew up way too fast!

Our greatest memories have always been vacationing together – those times are priceless to us and our hope is that you do the same with your families. God has given you life to enjoy. So, when you go to Flagstaff – look up at the stars so bright. Go to the movies, go bowling, the County Fair and fish in the pond. When you see the snow sparkling in the sunlight – remember God has given you the sight to see. Look around at the mountains, the sunsets and take in the smell of the ocean in the summer. God has given you these things as a beautiful gift!

Then, when the difficult times show up – you can thank Him for those, also, since you know He has a perfect plan for your life. Life is filled with seasons.

Consider it all joy, my brethren, when you encounter various trials, knowing that the testing of your faith produces endurance. (James 1:2-3)

He is using the tough things to produce endurance, so that you trust Him more and more each day. Each time you trust Him with something – He proves to you how trustworthy He really is.

On those days when the business seems to be falling apart or the children seem to want nothing to do with God – those are the days to smile and rejoice for throughout the years God has been preparing you. You can lay your head on the pillow at night knowing this:

HE IS FAITHFUL,
  HE LOVES YOU,
   HE HAS A PLAN FOR YOUR LIFE,
     HE IS CONSTANTLY MOVING YOU TO DIFFERENT
     PLACES…

And that is why you don't have to take life too seriously…

When Your Spouse Is Having A Bad Day... Give Them Their Space

Sometimes – we just have bad days. We wake up grouchy and it gets worse from there. The interesting thing is that on the day that one of us is having a bad day – the other is usually having a good day. God is so good that way. Those are the days that we have to step it up and be there as a support to our spouse.

Sometimes support means just sitting and talking; letting them vent and tell you about their frustrations. Many times they don't even want advice – they just want someone to listen to how they feel. At these times – always be a good listener. Other times – they might not want to talk about it and it is best to give them their space. A good night's sleep does the job most of the time.

There are times in a marriage when bad days turn into bad weeks and often times it can turn it to months. That is when your patience will be tested and yet as you continually pray for your spouse, you must learn to allow God to work out in their life whatever the problem is. If this continues – please get support from others who can step in and help. Make sure the person you are talking to is not fueling gossip and dissension in your marriage. Sometimes it is something between your spouse and God and it will be one of those growth times in their lives. Your job will be to just be there and be loving – refusing to nag and try to make them talk.

Be certain the tables will turn at some point in your marriage and you will be on the other side; sad, frustrated or depressed. That is just life and your spouse will be able to respond to you in the same manner you responded to them. You are a team and it is good to recognize that just like a football team – people do get injured. It is those times that the other team members have to work more diligently to keep the team going. Always remember…

THIS TOO SHALL PASS.

As you look back on these difficult times, you will learn that you cannot control your spouse and their emotions – but you can learn to trust God through these times!

When A Disagreement Is Over – Forget It. Our Mercies Must Be New Every Day

We are imperfect people living in an imperfect world. We will make mistakes and say hurtful things and unfortunately our spouse will feel the pain on the other end. However, what comes next is an important part of marriage – forgiveness and forgetfulness.

First, we must learn how to forgive. When Jesus died on the cross for our sins He did so to forgive us – to never count our transgressions against us. That is the picture we have to look at when it comes to our spouse – we must learn to wipe away the hurt we feel over harsh words or hurtful situations.

> **As far as the east is from the west, so far has He removed our transgressions from us. (Psalm 103:12)**

How do we do this? How do we forgive when we have been hurt so deeply? Maybe you were lied to or deceived. Maybe your feelings were hurt so severely that you are sure you will never forget what was said. Maybe you have lost a certain amount of trust in your marriage. Believe it or not – each day is a learning experience that usually does consist of working through even the most difficult situations including these just mentioned. We have to continually go back to the fact we are all human. We have our moments of saying and doing really stupid things. When this happens – we have to do what Jesus did for us and forgive. He knows our weaknesses and imperfections. That is what we must learn about our spouse – ***they are not perfect.***

Through it all you will grow together through the hurt and pain along with being able to work through the issues of "why".

Why did you do that?
Why did you hurt me or say those awful things?
Why are you distant and refuse to talk with me?
Why do you put more effort into work or school than
our marriage?
Why do you like to read novels instead of interacting
with me?
And then, you will be able to work through the "why's" of it all.
Talk through it.
Find out what the root of the problem is.

For many people, it is easier to keep quiet and to themselves than to try and talk about the problem. Do you get angry when confronted with something? Do you fly off the handle when your spouse it trying to talk with you about something that is bothering them? If you are responding in a negative way – it would make sense why they do not want to talk. You will have to learn how to receive your spouse's comments or concerns without an angry attitude. You will need to pray that God will give you a willing heart to do this with a heart of compassion and patience.

The story about the Prodigal son in **Luke 15:11-13** is a good example of how a father was deeply hurt over his son's actions, yet forgiveness reigned in the end. **"A man had two sons. The younger of them said to his father, 'Father, give me the share of the estate that falls to me.' So he divided his wealth between them. And not many days later, the younger son gathered everything together and went on a journey into a distant country, and there he squandered his estate with loose living."**

Just like the Prodigal son, people make mistakes. They think something will make them happy and, when it is all said and done, they realize how wrong they were. **Luke 15:14-17** goes on to say, **"Now when he had spent everything, a severe famine occurred in that country and he began to be impoverished. So he went and hired himself out to one of the citizens of that country, and he sent him into his fields to feed swine. And he would have gladly filled his stomach with the pods that the** swine were eating, and no one was giving anything to him. But when he came to his senses, he said, 'How many of my father's hired men have more than enough bread, but I am dying here with hunger!'"

Marriage is filled with moments when your spouse realizes his or her actions were hurtful or wrong. Sin has a way of bringing a person to their senses. When they do, and when they repent – that is when the healing can begin. When the Prodigal son returned home, the father was waiting with open arms. He could have been angry and held a grudge against his son forever but in this parable, forgiveness and moving on into the future to a renewed relationship with his son.

> I will get up and go to my father, and will say to him, "Father, I have sinned against heaven, and in your sight; I am no longer worthy to be called your son; make me as one of your hired men." So he got up and came to his father. But while he was still a long way off, his father saw him and felt compassion for him, and ran and embraced him and kissed him. And the son said to him, "Father, I have sinned against heaven and in your sight; I am no longer worthy to be called your son." But the father said to his slaves, "Quickly bring out the best robe and put it on him, and put a ring on his hand and sandals on his feet; and bring the fattened calf, kill it, and let us eat and celebrate; for this son of mine was dead and has come to life again; he was lost and has been found." And they began to celebrate. (Luke 15:18-24)

There is true and false repentance in a marriage. When your spouse is truly repentant, truly has a heart to change, and truly remorseful, then you will have the opportunity to rejoice over them just as the father was able to do for his son. The world will tell you the opposite. That you should be angry, never let them forget what they did to you, and hold a grudge forever. That is why it is important to know God and His Word so you will be able to do things in a godly way which will honor God and eventually bless you with a stronger, more intimate marriage.

The second part is forgetfulness which means never returning to that argument. That means refusing to bring up the past. That means moving on in our lives as we recognize that most things said out of anger aren't really our true feelings. It just may feel true at the moment in the heat of the argument.

> **Brethren, I do not regard myself as having laid hold of it yet; but one thing I do: forgetting what lies behind and reaching forward to what lies ahead, I press on toward the goal for the prize of the upward call of God in Christ Jesus.**
> **(Philippians 3:13-14)**

The Bible has the best advice – forget the past and reach forward to the future with a new knowledge of your spouse. Learn why there was a problem and see how you can help make it better. Discover how you can come along side of your spouse when difficulty arises and learn where the communication breakdown is. Look not only at your spouse but inside yourself and see if there is something you are doing that is causing the conflict in the situation. Be a better listener. Refuse to get angry. Be patient. Be kind. Use every situation to build a better, stronger foundation for your marriage.

> **Everyone who comes to Me and hears My words and acts on them, I will show you whom he is like: he is like a man building a house, who dug deep and laid a foundation on the rock; and when a flood occurred, the torrent burst against that house and**

**could not shake it, because it had been well
built. But the one who has heard and has
not acted accordingly, is like a man who
built a house on the ground without any
foundation; and the torrent burst against it
and immediately it collapsed, and the ruin
of that house was great.
(Luke 6:47-50)**

Trouble in your marriage isn't always bad…it helps you learn
about each other in order for your marriage to be built on a
strong foundation. Recognize that God wants you to grow in your
marriage and your relationship with Him. Conflict is the way we
learn. Trials are how we learn to trust God. You don't need to fall
apart when there is a problem. Spend the time needed to work
through it and find out what is at the bottom of the conflict. Only
then will you be able to move forward with a better knowledge
and understanding of your spouse.

**Then Peter came and said to Him, "Lord,
how often shall my brother sin against me
and I forgive him? Up to seven times?"
Jesus said to him, "I do not say to you, up
to seven times, but up to seventy times
seven." (Matthew 18:21-22)**

God Must Be Your Provider For Everything

When you get married, many things you thought you knew about your spouse will most likely change.

You might start thinking things like...

You always watched the movies I liked only to find out you really hated them.

You never got angry with me and now you seem angry all the time.

You were always so self confident and now you seem jealous and possessive.

You used to be so attentive and call me five times a day and now I only talk to you if I call.

We would always be together and now you spend your time without me.

The house was always clean and now it is not.

You used to want sex all the time and now you don't.

We used to laugh and have fun and now life seems difficult and stressful.

You used to not be worried about finances until we got married and now it is a constant worry.

Does any of this sound familiar?

Somehow before we got married our spouses were always on their best behavior. Then once the wedding ring was on, the "I Do's" were said and the honeymoon was over – the real person started emerging! That can be a shocking moment when you start to realize this person you married is a little different than the one you thought you were marrying! Rest assured this is normal. Somewhere in our lives we were given the "happily ever after story". The Princess and Prince were always compatible, always wanted to be together, and clearly had the same hopes and dreams. But, in reality – that doesn't happen. Marriage is work. Marriage is communication. Marriage is about giving and learning to care more for your spouse than yourself.

So, the point is this:

Your spouse will never be able to meet all your needs.

They will never be there for you at all times. They will never be able to comfort you in the way you need to be comforted. They will never be able to supply all your emotional requirements. God has to be your provider for all of these things. He is the only One who knows everything about you. He is the One you can go to for things like stress, doubt, worry, panic and fear. When you need encouragement or stability; He is there for you. When you need to feel truly loved – you will only have to pick up His Word and read about God's love and passion for you. It is only there that you will be truly satisfied in life. Our spouses will be there for us to a certain extent, but in reality – we need to go to the Maker and Creator for our needs. He is the One who knows what is best for us and in that we can be satisfied with whatever He brings in our lives.

Stressed about financial problems? God is the one who is your Provider and we need to learn to trust Him and not our pay checks.

Stressed about children? God is the Giver of children. He has given them to us, or not given them to us, for a purpose. We need to pray for them and entrust them to the one who created them.

Not getting along with your spouse? God is the only One who can change your spouse's heart. He is the One who transforms hearts, minds and actions. Our responsibility is to pray for them.

Fearful about the future? Trust your lives to the only One that holds the future. He created you, saved you and has a plan for you. The minute you stop trying to control things yourself is the moment you will begin to relax in your life. When you begin to realize that God is an awesome God who controls everything – then you will learn to trust Him instead of your spouse. Worried about your job? God is the One who makes straight your paths to put you where He wants you. Worried about getting pregnant? God is in control of when that will happen. Worried about the strained relationship with your spouse? God has to step in and change their lives. Worried about what will happen ten years from now? You have no control.

There is your answer…***You have no control, but God does.***

> **And we know that God causes all things to work together for good to those who love God, to those who are called according to His purpose. (Romans 8:28)**

All things…which will always include the difficult things like money problems, children problems, stress, heartache and just plain life. When you get this – your spouse will become less and less of an issue and you will look at life and your relationship on a completely different level. Instead of thinking you control everything – you can sit back and relax as you pray knowing that God is the One you need to turn to. He is the only One who can truly provide for you all that you will ever need.

> **The Lord is my rock and my fortress and my deliverer, My God, my rock, in whom I take refuge; My shield and the horn of my salvation, my stronghold. (Psalm 18:2)**

Be An Encourager

In your marriage, one of the most difficult things you will need to learn is how to be an encourager. We live in a world that is discouraging. Work is tough, the economy looks gloomy, the news is depressing and if we are not careful we can buy into the negativity the world has to offer.

It is easy in a marriage to get in the habit of being negative. Yet, it is the one place we need to make a conscious effort to be positive. We all need to be encouraged. We need to know our spouse is behind us in the things we do. We need encouragement that regardless of our job, our grades or what our kids are doing that it is all okay because we trust in God. We need to learn to put God back into the picture and re-focus our lives to be "God" centered and not Î¨¨¨"us" centered.

When Jesus was about to be crucified, He told Peter that he would deny Him three times. Jesus could have been angry with Peter and discouraged him about the decisions he was about to make, yet even in this difficult time He encouraged him knowing that in the end – God would use Peter in a mighty way.

> **But I have prayed for you, that your faith**
> **may not fail; and you, when once you have**
> **turned again, strengthen your brothers.**
> **(Luke 22:32)**

Jesus never made him feel like a failure or worthless – He encouraged him in the end to strengthen those around him.

Failure is not fatal and if your husband loses an account at work, or does something he shouldn't have – he needs to be encouraged by you. If your wife loses her temper with the kids she needs to know you understand, and will be there for her. You need to look at life with an encouraging heart. It is easy to make someone feel bad, yet your spouse needs to be uplifted, knowing you are the one person who will always have their back.

When we start to feel down and discouraged we need our spouse to be there to lift us up. We need uplifting words of encouragement and affirmation, because the more we are reminded that God is in control – the more encouraged about life we will become. We need encouraging words that will focus on an eternal perspective, and not a worldly one. We need to tell each other that everything is going to be okay.

Husbands

Your wife needs to know how much you appreciate her. She needs to be affirmed in how your house is clean and your laundry is done. She needs to verbally hear how nice she looks. She needs to feel honored as your wife and needs to know how much you appreciate her. If she is home all day with your children – you need to understand how difficult that is. You leave the house in the morning and are able to be with other adults at work while your wife is dealing with crying children who throw temper tantrums all day. That is probably the most difficult job in the world and you need to make sure she knows that you know how hard her job is. You need to spend extra money to make sure she has a babysitter a couple times during the week to give her time off. You would be amazed at how much having someone come clean your house once or twice a month would mean to her. She needs encouragement that she is still as beautiful and sexy to you as she was the day you got married. That takes time and words and action on your part to make her feel truly valued as your wife.

Wives

Your husband needs to know how much you appreciate him getting up early in the morning to go to work. He needs to know you are proud of him and you are his greatest advocate. As the man of the house, his stress is making sure you are taken care of financially and that weighs heavily on a man. He needs you to never make him feel bad for not making enough money. He needs you to be understanding if he has to work late or go on business trips. He needs you to be supportive in all he does because his work is how he provides for his family. He needs you to tell him how wonderful he is and on the days he is discouraged, he needs words of encouragement.

Your home might be the only source of peace, quiet and encouragement your husband will get all day. When the kids are asleep at night – your wife will need your undivided attention to reinforce your appreciation for her. The world can be a dark and dreary place and your home should be a place of uplifting and encouraging words. Facing tomorrow with the knowledge that your spouse is on your side and praying for you can make all the difference as you wake up to your same routine. Encouragement…

This is one of the most important elements to a happy marriage.

> **That is, that you and I may be encouraged together with you while among you, each of us by the other's faith, both yours and mine. (Romans 1:12)**

Remember There Are Seasons In Life

When you get married, you assume your life will always be the same and then when things change – it is confusing and frustrating. You used to feel in love all the time and now it doesn't feel the same. You used to have more money and now you don't. You used to be healthy and now something is wrong. You used to love life and now it seems unfair. You couldn't wait to have children and now they cry and whine all the time. You used to be able to go on vacation and now you can't afford it.

I used to…I used to…I used to

Solomon wrote in Ecclesiastes about this very thing. Life is filled with seasons and when you go into marriage recognizing this – when it starts to happen you will be prepared for it.

> **There is an appointed time for everything.**
> **And there is a time for every event under**
> **heaven—**
> **A time to give birth and a time to die;**
> **A time to plant and a time to uproot what**
> **is planted.**
> **A time to kill and a time to heal;**
> **A time to tear down and a time to build up.**
> **A time to weep and a time to laugh;**
> **A time to mourn and a time to dance.**
> **A time to throw stones and a time to**
> **gather stones;**
> **A time to embrace and a time to**
> **shun embracing.**
> **A time to search and a time to give up**
> **as lost;**
> **A time to keep and a time to throw away.**

A time to tear apart and a time to
sew together;
A time to be silent and a time to speak.
A time to love and a time to hate;
A time for war and a time for peace.
(Ecclesiastes 3:1-12)

Solomon understood this idea of change. God made sure this was written in His Word to us for a purpose. He doesn't want us to fall apart when life throws us a curve ball. He wants us to understand that part of living this life here on earth means there will be ups and downs. But through it all – He wants to be the constant straight line. He wants us to trust Him. To rest in Him. To hope in Him through the difficult days.

There will be times when you will love life and everything will be going your way. There will be times when the kids get along, the bills are being paid and you and your spouse are getting along. Then, one day, you will wake up to months of chaos when the kids fight, someone gets hurt and there are extra bills to pay and because money is tight you and your spouse seem to be arguing more than normal.

Welcome to the real world where things change daily...

One of the keys to handling change is our attitude. This is always a choice we have. We can look at the glass half empty or the glass half full. We can choose to be negative and angry and frustrated or we can choose to be joyful, positive and encouraging. What happens when you have to take a pay cut to keep the company going? What about when you are called to go out of town on a business trip? What about learning your wife is going out of town for a few days and you have to keep the kids? What if your wife gets sick and you have to change your schedule to help her?

All your life, there will be changes, yet we have a great opportunity to meet these times with a biblical concept. **James 1:2-3** says, **"Consider it all joy, my brethren, when you**

encounter various trials, knowing that the testing of your faith produces endurance."

Being joyful is a God given quality. If you do not have it, you need to be praying for joy independent of your circumstance. When you begin to understand that every day is a new adventure, then when things happen unexpectedly, you will be prepared.

You need to remember that as a married couple, you are a team. You will need to be there for each other. Through the difficult days, one spouse will be affected more and the other will have to pick up the slack. That is how it always will be, so just be prepared to always look at problems through an eternal viewpoint.

> **God always has a purpose.**
> **He will never leave you or forsake you.**
> **He is your only source of peace.**

Knowing this will help pull you through the ups and downs of life.

I Thee Wed

Rob & Lisa
September 1979

Gabby & Aaron
June 1999

To Love You Unconditionally

Rob & Val
July 2003

For Better Or For Worse

Sean & Brecken
June 2006

To Love And
To Cherish

Micah & Shayla
March 2009

To Have And To Hold

Jesse & Hannah
July 2009

As Long As We Both Shall Live

Cheyanne

Dusty

Being Strong Willed Will Hurt Your Marriage

Having a successful marriage will depend on how willing you are to give up your strong willed attitude. Usually having a strong will means you will always want to win the arguments, always want your own way and you will assume you are right most of the time. Recognizing this trait is the first step, and then looking for ways to overcome this character trait will be key to the success of your marriage. Unfortunately, marriages must be built on humility and caring for the other person more than yourself.

The person who has the strongest will must learn to take their eyes off of themselves and put them onto their spouse.

> **When pride comes, then comes dishonor,**
> **but with the humble is wisdom.**
> **(Proverbs 11:2)**

Pride is spoken of as dishonorable and humility is linked to wisdom. To have a peaceful marriage, the strong willed person will have to recognize that when they demand their own way they are operating in an ungodly manner. Humility is the way God calls marriage partners to live together.

Learning to put the other person first in all you do is something God will have to instill in your life. You must learn to care more for what your spouse wants than caring for yourself.

That could play out in a number of ways.

Who usually asks...

Where do you want to go out to eat?
    What movie do you want to watch?

What are your plans for the weekend?

Who is the one…

Who usually starts arguments?
 Who takes the longest to make it right?
   Who won't stop until they get their way?

Think about how great a marriage would be if both people were working from a state of humility and refusing to care about themselves above the other. Their focus in life would be to please the other person more than getting their own way. Think of how peaceful your home would be.

> **Whoever exalts himself shall be humbled; and whoever humbles himself shall be exalted. (Matthew 23:12)**

God has a funny way of teaching us how to be humble so it is best to learn this as soon as possible!

> **But He gives a greater grace. Therefore it says, "God is opposed to the proud, but gives grace to the humble." (James 4:6)**

> **To sum up, all of you be harmonious, sympathetic, brotherly, kindhearted, and humble in spirit; not returning evil for evil or insult for insult, but giving a blessing instead; for you were called for the very purpose that you might inherit a blessing. (1 Peter 3:8-9)**

Peter could not have said it better: live in harmony with each other, sympathize with your spouse, and be kind and humble. Don't get back at your spouse if they hurt you, but instead pray for them.

Someone gave us this description of what it means to die to ourselves. A great marriage would be one that both people would live by these principles.

DYING TO SELF IS…

When you are forgotten or neglected or purposely set as naught and you sting and hurt with the insult of oversight, but your heart is happy, being counted worthy to suffer for Christ.

When your good is evil spoken of, when your wishes are crossed, your advise disregarded, your opinions ridiculed and you refuse to let anger rise in your heart, or even defend yourself, but take it all in patient loving silence.

When you are content with any food, any offering, any raiment, any climate, any society, any attitude, any interruption by the will of God.

When you never care to refer to yourself in conversation, or to record your own good works, or itch after commendation, when you can truly love to be unknown.

When you see your brother prosper and have his needs met and can honestly rejoice with him in spirit and feel no envy nor question God while your own needs are far greater and in desperate circumstances.

When you can receive correction and reproof from one of one less stature than yourself, can humbly submit inwardly as well as outwardly, finding no rebellion or resentment rising up within your heart.

This is dying to self…

That is what a great marriage is made of.
That is what a great life is made of.

Men Need To
Take The
Lead Spiritually

Men have the most important job in the world and that is to lead their wife and child(ren) spiritually. The most difficult part of marriages we see, is when a wife wants to go to church, spend time in God's Word, get involved with a neighborhood small group and yet the husband has little desire to do any of these things. As a Christian we must remember that God says the greatest commandment is to love Him with all our heart, mind and soul. If you, as the husband, say you are a Christian and yet have little or no desire to do any of these things; then you need to do things out of an obedient heart before you might begin to ever "feel" anything.

> **Blessed is the man who listens to me, watching daily at my gates, waiting at my doorposts. (Proverbs 8:34)**

> **And let us consider how to stimulate one another to love and good deeds, not forsaking our own assembling together, as is the habit of some, but encouraging one another; and all the more as you see the day drawing near. (Hebrews 10:24-25)**

As the spiritual leader of your home, if you are to have any kind of spiritual impact on your household, you must do what this verse says-which means this is a daily occurrence. If you are going to impart spiritual wisdom to your children, then you will have to know God and His Word to have answers. We live in a difficult time and your spiritual leadership is desperately needed. Taking your family to church a couple times a month will never give them what they need to grow in their relationship with Christ. It is your job to make sure your wife and children are doing everything they can to grow in their faith.

As Christians, we do not have a choice to take this lightly. The Bible is filled with exhortations regarding how we are to live. God calls us to put Him first in all we do. If that is the case, then anything available to learn and grow in our relationship with Christ should always come first. You, as the man, are the key to your family's spiritual development.

If your wife sees you reading your Bible and praying; then she can trust that you are seeking godly wisdom for your family. She will be able to have the confidence that the decisions you are making in your household will be good, because you are seeking and trusting God for them. If your children are seeing you read your Bible, then they too will have faith that God is the most important part of your life. It is imperative that your family sees you, as the husband and father, taking on this role.

We see so many families where the mother is the spiritual leader and dad just goes along with what she wants to do. Unfortunately, the children can see straight through that and when it comes time for them to go to church or get involved they look to the father. If dad isn't really excited about anything spiritual then the kids won't be either. They have to see what a true, biblical, transformed Christian leader looks like; and they will always look to the head of the house ... which is the father.

If you don't feel like doing anything to encourage your personal relationship with Christ, our suggestion is for you to take the step to do it anyway. That could mean picking up your Bible in the morning or at night and reading a few verses. That might mean making a stand to be at church regardless of how you wake up feeling. That could mean joining a small group to be with other believers or listening to sermons of pastors you like on the way to work. That could mean keeping a Christian book in the bathroom to read.

Make the things of God a priority! On weekends – there are so many distractions: the lake, the football game, hunting, fishing or the dance recitals. There are basketball and soccer games, Little League, paint-balling and snowboarding. All our lives we will have to determine what matters the most – a sports event, that won't matter ten years from now, or showing our children that God must always come first. Our children must see that our relationship with God is the most important part of our lives. They are watching us and if they see us reading our Bible, going to church and going to Bible studies then what is important to us will also be important to them as they grow up. Your example will be "heard" more clearly than your words.

In this fast paced day and age we live in, our minds are filled with everything except God. The longer we wait, the more difficult it becomes and the kids are grown and gone without a biblical foundation. God says in **Proverbs 22:6, "Train up a child in the way he should go, even when he is old he will not depart from it."** That is a clear command from God that our duty is to train our children to know God and His Word! Yet, if we, as the husband and father are not doing that, we cannot expect our children ever will either.

> **Listen, O my people, to my instruction; Incline your ears to the words of my mouth. I will open my mouth in a parable; I will utter dark sayings of old, which we have heard and known, and our fathers have told us. We will not conceal them from their children, but tell to the generation to come the praises of the Lord, and His strength and His wondrous works that He has done. For He established a testimony in Jacob and appointed a law in Israel, which He commanded our fathers that they should teach them to their children, that the generation to come might know, even the children yet to be born, that they may arise and tell them to their children, that they should put their**

**confidence in God and not forget the works
of God, but keep His commandments, and
not be like their fathers, a stubborn and
rebellious generation, a generation that did
not prepare its heart and whose spirit was
not faithful to God. The sons of Ephraim
were archers equipped with bows, yet they
turned back in the day of battle. They did
not keep the covenant of God and refused
to walk in His law; they forgot His deeds
and His miracles that He had shown them.
(Psalm 78:1-11)**

This life we live here on earth is short and yet the Bible says
eternity is forever! Therefore, we should be more concerned for
the eternal things in our lives. Jobs come and go. Houses come
and go. Sports teams come and go. Yet, God wants us to live
our lives here on earth with a purpose to know Him and serve
Him. In the verses above it talks about a tragic situation – one
generation sees the incredible work and hand of God and yet
other generations go by without ever hearing. If we aren't there to
teach our children, they will be part of a stubborn and rebellious
generation that will not prepare their heart and who will not be
faithful to God. This has to be passed down from one generation
to another or our children, grand children and great grand
children will never come to know Christ and will not spend
eternity in heaven. Eternal things must be our highest goal in life.

If you do not have the desire to grow in your faith – find a good
men's study or meet with someone you respect once a week who
will challenge you to be the husband and father God has meant
for you to be. You are the key in your family to raise children who
will love and seek God for their own lives. Our hope and prayer
is that you will take the challenge and make a decision to live for
Christ with a full heart. That will require action on your part. If
you do not want to – then pray desperately that God will give you
the desire to know Him more and move forward anyway. The
next generation, your children, are counting on you to lead your
family so they will know how to lead theirs.

*Always Build
Your Spouse Up
In Front
Of Others*

Because all of you boys were so close in age it was inevitable that when you would get together there would be someone you would antagonize. The best day, for us as parents, was watching this dynamic when you would bring your wives into the picture and we were blessed and thankful to see the outcome. Your wives would always take your side and take a stand against any brotherly opposition. Instead of going along with everyone when they were making fun of you – your wives would stick up for you and we began to realize how important that is in a marriage.

As a married couple you need to remember God calls you "one flesh" which means you both are a team. When one feels hurt or threatened the other one, who is part of you, should have your back. Your spouse needs to always feel the impact of your love, especially when others are not being that nice. They need to know – out loud – that you are on their side and will stand beside you regardless.

A second part to this is making sure you never downgrade or disagree with your spouse in front of other people. So many times we see one spouse actually arguing over the smallest thing in front of others. We are all human, and our memories are leaving us daily, but it is very disrespectful to call out your spouse in front of others. If Dad says something happened a year ago and I told everyone out loud that it was really ten months ago then it makes Dad look stupid in front of other people. If Mom says something about the kids when they were younger and my recollection isn't the same I don't correct her in front of others. It is a really bad habit that we see many couples doing.

If your spouse says something that is not how you remember it – do not ever address it in public. Nothing is that big of a deal that your spouse needs to be embarrassed over. Part of this is the feeling we always have to be right all the time and somehow correcting our spouse makes us feel better about ourselves. Please remember that this is a very destructive pattern that can hurt your spouse and those listening around you. Be very careful in public how you treat them.

Another thing to be very careful of is what you tell others about the money your husband makes. Men take such pride in being able to provide for their family and the worst thing you can do is downgrade his pay. That can be done in many ways. It can be as simple as "I can't go with you, we can't afford it" or "I wish we could buy what you have but we don't have the money." Even the smallest remarks can make a man feel like he is not providing for his family in the manner he would like to.

Your spouse must know that you are their greatest fan. When their whole world seems to be falling apart they need the reassurance that regardless, you will always be on their side. As you grow older together, life changes drastically and with the changes your spouse needs to know you are in it for the long haul. When bad times arise – they need to know you will stick with them through thick and thin. You are one flesh and nothing can tear you apart. Making sure others know how much your spouse means to you is an important element in your marriage.

That is something we all need to be reminded of...

If you are having a difficult time with your spouse, it is easy to talk bad about them to others. You undoubtedly will feel the need to vent your feelings and your frustrations about what is going on. Unfortunately, the more you talk - the worse you feel toward your spouse. If you truly are having problems – find a person to talk to that will help you through the rough patch who will give you good, biblical advice. Many times that needs to be someone outside your friendship circle – someone who can be very discerning. Most of your friends will always take your side without being able to see the whole picture and therefore you will need to talk with someone who is very discerning and godly.

Remember this: the world will always think differently than what the Bible says. God has the wisdom needed to make your marriage work and it will take work on your part to study His Word for that. Be very careful with the words you say to others about your spouse. This too can be a very destructive habit.

Choose Your
Words Wisely

Be very careful with the words you use. What you say can be incredibly hurtful and words are very difficult to take back. If you know your spouse struggles in a certain area – do not continually antagonize them with what you say. **James 3:7-10 says, "For every species of beasts and birds, of reptiles and creatures of the sea, is tamed and has been tamed by the human race. But no one can tame the tongue; it is a restless evil and full of deadly poison. With it we bless our Lord and Father, and with it we curse men, who have been made in the likeness of God; from the same mouth come both blessing and cursing. My brethren, these things ought not to be this way."**

What we say can either hurt or heal our spouse. Be very careful to think about what you say before you say it, for with our words we can be a blessing or a curse. Think about the things you say on a daily basis. Are they words of encouragement and comfort or are they words that demean and hurt?

A great marriage is built on learning when to say certain things. If you have had a bad day then your spouse should know not to bring up something that is bothering them until a different time. If you know your spouse is better to talk about things in the morning, then get up and talk then. Always have the other person in mind when making those decisions. A big part of marriage is timing; learning to know when and how to have a discussion.

A wonderful marriage is built on learning how to communicate and that involves not living based on your emotions and feelings. Most of the time, you will need a good night's sleep in order to get a fresh perspective. Therefore, try really hard to not start deep discussions late at night. That brings on further stress and turmoil for the next day which snowballs into more frustration because you have added a lack of sleep on top of everything.

Sometimes you will need to hold in what you want to talk about until the weekend or schedule a time when you both will be able to calmly talk without the added stress of the work day and fussing children. You may need to schedule a date night where you can have each other's undivided attention to talk about what is bothering you. The biggest part to this is prayer. Women are emotional and process things differently than men do. So, for a woman you might want to give it a few days to pray about before you talk because in those few days – your feelings could change.

When you do start talking – be careful of the words you use. "You did this" or "you did that" tends to be very condemning and usually makes things worse. It would be helpful if you started with "I am feeling this way" or "I am struggling with something you said." Start with your feelings about a matter instead of accusing the other person. When talking, try to stay very calm. When you are working through issues you need to make sure it is a righteous, godly conversation. There is never a need to scream and shout and yell – you need to be guided by the Holy Spirit at all times, even when there is turmoil.

> **A gentle answer turns away wrath, but a harsh word stirs up anger. (Proverbs 15:23)**
>
> **A man has joy in an apt answer, and how delightful is a timely word! (Proverbs 15:1).**
>
> **The heart of the righteous ponders how to answer, but the mouth of the wicked pours out evil things. (Proverbs 15:28)**

Most arguments are just misunderstandings. They just need to be talked through.

It is very important to remember that God uses all things – even disagreements - to conform you to His image. Your best bet is to learn this early in your marriage. One of the greatest things our parents taught us growing up was: *If you don't have anything nice to say – don't say anything at all!* That is something that is still a valuable concept today – if what is going to come out of your mouth is not uplifting, nice and helpful then it is wise to keep your mouth shut until something nice does come out!

The sooner you learn how to communicate in a loving and honorable manner – the easier your marriage will be.

Care About The Things That Are Important To Your Spouse

Since you were raised in two different homes and environments there will inevitably be different things that are important to each of you. Thankfully for me (Mom), Dad has never been overly concerned about a home cooked meal each night and a spotless house to come home to. Because of our schedules, we are on the road more than at home and Dad has adjusted to just stopping by somewhere to pick up dinner. Thankfully for me (Dad) I tend to care mostly about having clean socks and T-shirts in my drawer in the mornings and Mom does her best to make sure that happens.

As you grow in your marriage you will find out what your spouse truly cares about.

Do they care about…

A clean house?
  Laundry put away?
    Dinner on the table when they get home?
      Sex a certain number of times a week?

What about…

The grass being mowed?
  The bed made in the morning?
    The dishes cleaned at night?
      Clean towels in the bathroom?
        Dirty clothes put away in the laundry room?

For each of us, it is our job to find out what upsets our spouse and make it a point to not do whatever that is. Think what a wonderful marriage it would be if two people would spend their time making sure their spouse's needs were taken care of before theirs. Many people live their married lives without concern for the other person, and yet, a great marriage consists of doing whatever we can to accommodate the other person.

Does your husband come home to a messy house while you are reading a book?

Does your wife come home to an unattended lawn while you are watching a sports game?

Do you hang out with your friends when your wife needs you to fix things around the house?

Do you shop when your husband asks you to stay on a budget?

As you can see, sometimes the little things are what start the arguments. If you know the yard or the house will upset your spouse then make it a point to do those things first. If sex and making dinner is important to them, then make it a point to make that happen. A marriage must be about meeting your spouse's needs and desires. This can be difficult to do sometimes. It takes communication to determine what is important to each other. Talk about it and ask them what it is they would like to see when they come home. We can guarantee that once you implement this into your life – you will have a more peaceful, less stressful marriage.

Jealousy And Possessiveness Can Destroy Your Marriage

When you get married, part of that process will be learning how to trust one another. Building trust is one of the most important elements of your relationship. Nothing will destroy your relationship faster than a jealous and possessive heart. When you get married, the bond you build will be one that encompasses trusting your spouse. There is nothing worse than having the one you love distrust what you are doing and who you are with during the day.

When your spouse is not responding to your phone calls, the first thought in your mind should always be positive, knowing they must be somewhere they cannot reach the phone. When you call their work and learn they are not there, your first reaction should never be wondering who they are with and why weren't you told. When they are speaking with someone of the opposite sex, your first response should never be "why are you talking with that person?" or "what did you say to them?" There should be enough love and trust between the two of you that you automatically know that if you are not getting a response on the other end – there is always a good reason why.

In order to make sure this does not happen, it is important to keep your lines of communication open. You need to let each other know where you will be and what you will be doing for the day – not because you are afraid they don't trust you, but out of a courtesy to your spouse. For Mom, I (Dad) always tell her what meetings I have for the day so in case she needs me there will never be any worry on her part. It is important to her that she knows how to get a hold of me if she needs to, and out of my love for her I want to ease her mind. If she can't find me during the day, she automatically knows that something came up and I will call her when I can and that has been built by over-communicating.

Here are some possessive and jealous comments that will hurt your marriage…

Why aren't you answering your phone?
Why were you late coming home?
Who were you talking to after work?
Why did you not call me today?
Who did you go to lunch with today?
Did you talk to that girl in your office today?
Who do you sit next to when you go to class?

There is a difference between asking questions to have a conversation versus asking questions with an accusing tone in your voice. If you are just curious about their day and who is in their class or workplace – that is fine but the line is crossed when your spouse begin to feel interrogated. You have to have a solid relationship with one another so that it wouldn't matter who they spoke to during the day because you know their heart belongs to you.

There is nothing worse than …

Living with someone who does not trust you.

Feeling you have to always be on guard with who you talk to.

Living in fear that you do not hear the phone when your spouse calls.

Worrying what your spouse is doing during the day.

Guard against this at all costs. Let your spouse know if they are being possessive or jealous and talk through ways to make that better. Marriage is difficult enough without the added stress of living in fear, worrying what your spouse is thinking all the time.

Ultimately, this could be a reflection on your trust in God. If you believe He has brought you together then you will have to learn to trust Him with all the outside influences that come into your lives on a daily basis. God is the protector of your heart and your mind and the more you focus on Him – the more peaceful you will be as your spouse walks out the door in the morning.

Make sure when you are concerned for your spouse's whereabouts, it is not because you are being possessive and jealous, but instead you are just concerned for them.

Work Through Problems Together

Many people struggle in their marriage because they do not understand the importance of working through issues together as a team. When you have a problem at home or at work – it is best to find time at the end of the day to talk through what has happened over the last 24 hours. The problems usually arise when the busyness of life takes over and there is no time to talk. We have always made it a habit that when we get home from our day – we sit down and discuss what has gone on during the day so if there are work issues or home issues that need to be dealt with – we can do this together.

The word "together" is the key. The problem starts when I (Mom) think I can handle everything at home by myself and Dad thinks he can handle the issues at work by himself. At that point we start walking down a single lane path and our lives become divided. To stay on that same path together – it takes time to keep each other informed. It takes time even when you are exhausted at the end of the day to share the highlights so communication is always happening. When you have an issue that needs to be dealt with – two suggestions come to mind.

First, for the men: be very careful to never "lord" it over your wife. Many men tell their wives what *they* are going to do because they have this "I am the man of the house" attitude. What happens is they spend their lives alienating their wives instead of including them. Women hate that. When a man comes across with that attitude – it only produces frustration and destroys a woman's self esteem. You, as the husband, need to remember that your marriage is not a "one man show" but both of you need to work together side by side.

Men, listen to your wives! Women need to feel that their input is important. They need to feel their opinions and thoughts are valuable, so make sure your heart – as a man – is to include your wife in all the decisions. Let her know how highly you esteem her input on your life and your decisions. Women tend to think differently on issues and it takes both – the heart and the mind to make intelligent, wise decisions.

Second, for the women: respect your husband's decision! It is easy to get frustrated when your husband does not take your advice and do what you think he should; but remember that the final decision is theirs to make. We must be praying consistently that God will give them the wisdom they need and then we need to turn it over to God, trusting their decision is from Him. Remember – your job is always to respect your husband and many times that will include respecting his decisions even if you disagree.

When we get a really high view of God and recognize His control over the situations in our lives, it becomes easier to trust our husbands. We know God is the One who can change a heart and a mind and if God **doesn't** change their heart or mind then we must relax knowing God is still in the midst of it all. We are all a "work in progress" and we will make many mistakes during our lifetime. We need to give each other the freedom to make those mistakes and grow from them. God is not going to let you down if your spouse makes a wrong move. God is the ultimate Chess Player and for every wrong move that your spouse makes – God has a move that can override what he or she has done.

God is constantly teaching us new things about ourselves, our spouse and Himself. His goal is to make us look more and more like Him each day with the same qualities of Jesus – patient, humble, caring more for others, and giving up our lives to serve others. Sometimes that is taught to us as we humbly, lovingly, trust and respect our husband's decisions even if we disagree. They need to know we stand behind them. They need to know we trust God for the decisions they make.

If things don't turn out the way your husband thought it would – never, ever use the words "I told you so." That is so damaging to a man's self esteem. As a team working together, if the quarterback makes a wrong decision and it loses the game for them – the worst thing he needs to hear is that it is his fault. Pray for them. Pray that they learn the lesson God wants to teach them. Maybe they ran ahead of God. Maybe they were refusing to wait on God and His timing. Your husband will have to learn those lessons on his own and when he falls – he needs you to let him know it is okay because regardless of what they do – **our trust is in God**. Life is a journey where the two of you are working through issues together. Look to each other for advice and support and remember to give each other a break. Take the time to talk through issues. Pray, love each other, be respectful, and then trust God alone for the outcome. You will be amazed at how easy this really is!

Marriage Is
A Commitment

When you get married, there will be a lot of emotional feelings regarding your spouse. You will feel emotions rise up when you see them or when they hold your hand. That is how it should be, but the problem begins when those emotional feelings tend to lessen or go away. When that happens your first response will be, "What is wrong with me? Am I falling out of love with the person I married?" and the answer you will need to know is "absolutely not!"

We have been married for over thirty years and we would say we love each other more now than we ever did when we first said "I Do" to each other. Our love is stronger and deeper and much more solid the older we get and the reason for that is our love is based on what love really is – a commitment – not a feeling.

If you think about what the Bible says love is in 1 Corinthians 13:4-7, emotional feelings do not have much to do with it. Think about this:

> **Patience, kindness, and refusing to be jealous takes commitment, not a feeling.**
> **Refusing to brag, be arrogant, act unbecomingly or seek our own is a commitment, not a feeling.**
> **Refusing to provoke or take into account a wrong suffered is a commitment, not a feeling.**
> **Refusing to rejoice in unrighteousness and determining in your heart to rejoice in the truth is a commitment, not a feeling.**
> **Bearing all things, believing all things, hoping all things and enduring all things is a commitment, not a feeling.**

Why? Because naturally we are not patient or kind. Naturally our emotions can produce jealousy and arrogance. In our flesh we want to hold on to hurt. Emotionally we want to care more for ourselves and not our spouse.

But the Bible says love is different - not an emotion, but a dedication and a loyalty. It takes a determination – not emotion – to be kind when we would rather not. It takes fortitude in our marriage to believe in one another and endure the hardships in life. If you are basing your relationship on feelings – you will be doomed from the start.

Feelings and emotions are normal and you should have them but the ultimate anchor to your marriage will always be commitment. Regardless of feelings – for they will come and go – you are committed to this person until the day you die. You are faithful to your vows. You are dedicated to your spouse. That is what true love is and the sooner you recognize this – your marriage will take on a whole new meaning. You will not be frightened or fearful when you don't "feel" like you did before, but instead you will relish in the fact you are growing a much stronger, deeper relationship. You will recognize that true, biblical love is not all about your emotions but something far greater.

The world system and the media will always depict love as something unbiblical. We see intense feelings and emotions in the movies, magazines, books and television shows. The problem is that true love – the kind of love that God has created – is not being portrayed in any of these. Without the knowledge of God's Word – we would be left in confusion wondering what is wrong with us. With the understanding God has given us – we can rest assured knowing that love is much, much, more than what we are being taught by the world.

Frustrated by the lack of emotions in your marriage? You can sit back and relax, knowing now that God has designed you for something superior – a love that is based on deep roots which will produce a strong union. When the storms of life come, you will be rooted and grounded and nothing can uproot you because you know the truth.

Love – true love – biblical love - a committed love

Nothing is more satisfying in life.

> **Love is patient, love is kind and is not jealous; love does not brag and is not arrogant, does not act unbecomingly; it does not seek its own, is not provoked, does not take into account a wrong suffered, does not rejoice in unrighteousness, but rejoices with the truth; bears all things, believes all things, hopes all things, endures all things. (1 Corinthians 13:4-7)**

Serving Others

So much of our lives revolve around ourselves. We are so dedicated to making sure our wants and desires are more important than anyone else's. We say things like: You hurt **my** feelings. **I** am so tired. **I** don't feel like doing that. **My** life is miserable. You never do what **I** want. **I** work so hard. You never listen to **me**.

And this goes on and on…

In life, so often it is easy to focus ourselves on what is important to us without regard for others. Yet, the Bible says the way to true happiness is getting our eyes off ourselves and serving others. When you find yourself in the self pity, self serving mode – recognize it is time to get out of that pit and start focusing on helping people!

God has a purpose for our lives which is to show others the love of Christ. The problem is that in order for that to happen – we need to get out of our comfort zones and as the Nike saying goes "Just Do It"! There are so many ways to shift our focus from ourselves to serving others. The community and church are great places to start. Find out what you like to do and what you are gifted in and then go do it. You will then start seeing a world outside of yourself that is in desperate need of the love of Christ. Your problems will become less and less as you focus on the hurts and heartaches of others.

Here are some examples:

> *Work at a homeless shelter.*
> *Serve food at a soup kitchen.*
> *Build homes in Mexico.*

Play an instrument in the church band.
Work with groups such as Feed My Starving
Children or World Vision.
Teach a small group.
Teach the Jr. High or High School kids at
your church.
Sing in the choir.
Help your neighbor mow his lawn.
Take food to someone who is hurting.
Help out at a nursing home.
Work in the inner city.
Collect shoes and jackets for the homeless.

The world is a big place with a lot of big problems! We, as the body of Christ, are called to engage in this life to help others. When you do that, you will notice a shift in your life. You will be less and less focused on your problems and more and more focused on helping others. We need to remember that we are the hands and feet of Jesus.

'For I was hungry, and you gave Me something to eat; I was thirsty, and you gave Me something to drink; I was a stranger, and you invited Me in; naked, and you clothed Me; I was sick, and you visited Me; I was in prison, and you came to Me.' "Then the righteous will answer Him, 'Lord, when did we see You hungry, and feed You, or thirsty, and give You something to drink? 'And when did we see You a stranger, and invite You in, or naked, and clothe You? 'When did we see You sick, or in prison, and come to You?' "The King will answer and say to them, 'Truly I say to you, to the extent that you did it to one of these brothers of Mine, even the least of them, you did it to Me.' (Matthew 25:35-40)

Take One Day
At A Time

It is easy to be fearful of the future. We worry about what will happen tomorrow, next week or next year. Yet, Jesus gave us a command about how to live a peaceful existence. What He calls us to do is this: refuse to worry.

> "For this reason I say to you, do not be worried about your life, as to what you will eat or what you will drink; nor for your body, as to what you will put on. Is not life more than food, and the body more than clothing? "Look at the birds of the air, that they do not sow, nor reap nor gather into barns, and yet your heavenly Father feeds them. Are you not worth much more than they? "And who of you by being worried can add a single hour to his life? "And why are you worried about clothing? Observe how the lilies of the field grow; they do not toil nor do they spin, yet I say to you that not even Solomon in all his glory clothed himself like one of these. "But if God so clothes the grass of the field, which is alive today and tomorrow is thrown into the furnace, will He not much more clothe you? You of little faith! "Do not worry then, saying, 'What will we eat?' or 'What will we drink?' or 'What will we wear for clothing?' "For the Gentiles eagerly seek all these things; for your heavenly Father knows that you need all these things. "But seek first His kingdom and His righteousness, and all these things

**will be added to you. "So do not worry
about tomorrow; for tomorrow will care
for itself. Each day has enough trouble of
its own. (Matthew 6:25-35)**

One day we were reading these verses and it dawned on us that
Jesus does not ever want us to worry about tomorrow. If that is
the case – how do we do that?

We came up with a funny idea. We decided to pretend that at
midnight each night we are going to die! So, if we are worried
about how something will play out the next day – we refuse to do
so because if in fact we die – we wouldn't be here for whatever we
were worried about!

As amusing as that seems – it actually works. It has become a joke
for us and when we start talking about what might happen the
next day we end up saying: "since we are dying tonight I guess it
doesn't really matter about tomorrow. If we do in fact wake up,
then God will give us everything we need to make it through
another 24 hour period."

Think about living life in that manner. No stress. No fear. God
controls what happens to us and worrying about it would never
change it anyway. Seeking God is the key. If we are seeking what
He wants for our lives then He will make sure we are taken care
of. That is how to stay stress free and worry free in your marriage.
Live one day at a time. Pretend the clock ends at midnight, and
should God decide to give you another day to live then He
will give you the wisdom and guidance to make it through that
day also.

**Surely goodness and loving kindness will
follow me all the days of my life, and I will
dwell in the house of the Lord forever.
(Psalm 23:6)**

This is the day which the Lord has made;

Let us rejoice and be glad in it.
(Psalm 118:24)

A Letter From
Mana And
Papa Boo

To all our children and grandchildren,

Papa Boo and I wanted to add a little something to the end of this book. As you know we have been married for over 50 years and so we wanted to just tell you why we think it has worked for us to have been married for this length of time.

Papa Boo and I are really different in our likes and dislikes when you get right down to it. He loves riding horses and I don't. He loves football and I don't. I like to shop and decorate. He doesn't. I like to stay in 5 star hotels and he likes to travel in the motor home. I guess we could go on and on, but what I'm getting at is we give in to one another a lot of the time. I went to horse shows and traveled in the motor home all across the United States. It wasn't really what I wanted to do, but it enabled our 2 daughters to have a love of horses and they showed right along with their dad. So, that was a good thing keeping the girls busy.

Football games were at ASU for many years. In fact, I was pregnant when we started going to the ASU games and now it is the Cardinals games. We tailgated many times because it was something Papa Boo liked to do. I can remember getting up a 4am to mix eggs and half and half in gallon containers to take to the Fiesta Bowl game and serve breakfast for 25 people or more. It was something Papa Boo liked to do and visit with many business friends. Me, I would have probably liked to have slept in and have him go to the game without me. So, sometimes we did the things we really didn't want to do, but we were together. That is the most important thing and it made him love me more. He, in turn, didn't mind if I spent money on maintenance for myself such as hair, skin, pedicures and nail appointments. So, it works both ways.

I can't tell you enough how important RESPECT is for each other. Papa Boo has always made me feel important and treated me like a queen. He still brings home bouquets of flowers for me to enjoy. Even though he has worked all day and no matter how tired he is, he thinks to stop by the grocery store and bring home a dozen roses to me. How thoughtful is that! It wouldn't have to be a dozen roses, one would do. It is the thought that counts.

Another very important thing is to never go to sleep mad! I know you've probably heard that before, but think about it, what if something happened to your spouse during the night and you had gone to bed mad. You would have to live with that for the rest of your life. Not a pretty thing.

Papa Boo kisses me every morning before leaving for the office and he gives me a kiss when he comes home for dinner at night. Another plus in my eyes. He tells me how good the meals are even when I've tried a new recipe that really didn't turn out well. He didn't want to hurt my feelings knowing I spent a lot of time preparing it. We still hold hands when we're out. We just enjoy being close to each other. He has never felt superior over me and he still makes me feel like I'm the most beautiful woman in the world even when I look my worst.

So, these are just a few things that deserve to be mentioned in this letter to all of you. It's not how much money you have, but how much you love one another. Hold on to that love. It's hard to find today.

Bringing your children up in a Christian home is so important. Get those little kids in church early on. What better way for them to begin their lives than knowing that there is a GOD who is looking after them.

That's about it! I'm sure there are many more things that we could mention, but these are some of the most important in our eyes.

We love all of you and just want you to be as happy as we have been!

Mana and Papa Boo

June 1957

In Conclusion

Love God
  Love one another
    Have fun together
      Laugh together
        Enjoy each day
          Forgive each other promptly
            Forget quickly
Disagree in love
    Respect each other
      Enjoy the role God has given you
        Forget the past
          Look to the future
            Trust God for everything
              Remember life is filled with seasons
Run from temptation
    Guard your eyes
      Pick your battles wisely
        Learn from your mistakes
          Rely on God as your Provider
            Be an encourager

Appreciate your spouse
    Refuse to be strong willed
      Men – lead your family spiritually
        Pray consistently for your spouse
          Build up your spouse in front of others
            Always have your spouse's back.

Choose your words carefully
    Care more for your spouse's feelings than your own
      Get out and serve – give your life away to others
        Refuse to be jealous

Make your ear attentive to wisdom, incline your heart to understanding. (Proverbs 2:2)

For wisdom will enter your heart and knowledge will be pleasant to your soul. (Proverbs 2:10)

How blessed is the man who finds wisdom and the man who gains understanding. (Proverbs 3:13)

The conclusion, when all has been heard, is: fear God and keep His commandments, because this applies to every person. (Ecclesiastes 12:13)